300

Incredible Things

for Self-Help & Wellness

on the

Internet

300INCREDIBLE.COM, LLC
600 Village Trace, Building 23
Marietta, Georgia 30067

(800) 909-6505

ISBN 1-930435-00-2

Introduction

No matter how good our lives are, or how well-adjusted we appear to be, there is always room for improvement. This book provides you with resources that can assist you in all situations. Sit back, take a deep breath and surf the Web to a better existence.

Dr. Ed Rubenstein
edrub@mindspring.com
http://www.sages-way.com

Ken Leebow
Leebow@300INCREDIBLE.COM
http://www.300INCREDIBLE.com

Notice

This book lists what we believe to be interesting and useful self-help and wellness sites on the Internet. We have not tried to determine the correctness or completeness of the information contained on these sites. Therefore, the sites included should be used for general educational purposes only, and each individual should consult with his or her own certified health professional for all specific advice related to self-help and wellness.

— Dedication —

To all those who have committed themselves
to helping others be the best they can be.

About the Authors

Dr. Ed Rubenstein, psychologist and author, has provided services in various hospital, university and community settings since 1978. People from all walks of life have gained significant benefits from his teachings, and he also serves as a corporate and human development consultant. Ed's workshops in the areas of Performance Enhancement, Wellness, Stress Management, Relationship Building and Self-Mastery have been enthusiastically received. This book and his recently-released volume, "An Awakening from the Trances of Everyday Life: A Journey to Empowerment," are outgrowths of his dedication to the fields of self-improvement and wellness.

Ed enjoys living in the Blue Ridge Mountains with his wife and two sons. When he is not working or volunteering, you will often find Ed playing with his sons, strolling through the mountains or sitting by the river and admiring nature.

Ken Leebow has been involved with the computer business for over twenty years. The Internet has fascinated him since he began exploring it several years ago, and he has helped over a million readers utilize its resources. Ken has appeared frequently in the media, educating individuals about the Web's greatest hits. He is considered a leading expert on what is incredible about the Internet.

When not online, you can find Ken playing tennis, running, reading or spending time with his family. He is living proof that being addicted to the Net doesn't mean giving up on the other pleasures of life.

Acknowledgments

Putting a book together requires many expressions of appreciation. The following people deserve our special thanks:

- Ed's family—wife Paramjit and sons Arun and Sage—who recognized the importance of this work and provided encouragement, and brother Al Rubenstein and associate Julie Parker who provided support throughout this project.

- Ken's family—Denice, Alissa and Josh—for being especially supportive during the writing of the book.

- Paul Joffe and Janet Bolton, of *TBI Creative Services*, for their editing and graphics skills.

- Mark Krasner and Janice Caselli for sharing the vision of the book and helping make it a reality.

The Incredible Internet Book Series

300 Incredible Things to Do on the Internet • Volume I

300 More Incredible Things to Do on the Internet • Volume II

300 Incredible Things for Kids on the Internet

300 Incredible Things for Sports Fans on the Internet

300 Incredible Things for Golfers on the Internet

300 Incredible Things for Travelers on the Internet

300 Incredible Things for Health, Fitness & Diet on the Internet

300 Incredible Things for Auto Racing Fans on the Internet

300 Incredible Things for Self-Help & Wellness on the Internet

300 Incredible Things to Learn on the Internet

America Online Web Site Directory
Where to Go for What You Need

TABLE OF CONTENTS

TABLE OF CONTENTS (continued)

CHAPTER I
HELP YOURSELF

1
Help Your Self

http://www.selfgrowth.com

A guide for self-improvement and self-help that includes weekly newsletters, articles and a message board.

2
Psych Central

http://www.psychcentral.com/web.htm

Dr. John Grohol's Mental Health Page has it all: an abundance of self-help, psychology and mental health resources.

3
Building Better Lives

http://www.vow.com
Here you will find lots of useful information about living well; from healthy body and personal growth to a healthy workplace.

4
Meaningful Living

http://www.lifementoring.com
Enjoy inspirational and motivational quotes of great thinkers and find articles on personal development.

5
Self-Help for You

http://www.helpself.com
A fun site for learning about a variety of personal growth topics. How about taking a quiz to assist you with self-discovery?

6
Queendom

http://www.queendom.com
Take a variety of personality, intelligence and health-related tests. There are also plenty of personal stories, articles and an advice column for you to explore.

7
Favorite Places

http://www.bhglive.com/scgi/guide/UserGuide.cgi
Better Homes and Gardens has created a collection of favorite places on the Internet with lots of excellent sites on education, health, parenting, kids, gardening, money, crafts and more.

8
Help Has Arrived

http://www.4selfhelp.com
This self-help site can help you find what you are looking for.

9
Mindtools
http://www.mindtools.com
Explore an assortment of articles on such topics as managing stress, time management, problem solving, improving memory, goal setting, communication skills and sports psychology.

10
Spirituality and Health
http://www.spiritualityhealth.com
This site can help you learn about yourself and enhance your relationships, so you may have a more fulfilling and meaningful life.

11
Cyber Psych
http://www.cyber-psych.com
Stop here to get professional psychological information. You will be guided to appropriate links for an assortment of mental health categories.

12
Be Positive
http://www.positiveprojections.com
Are you tired of all the negativity? This is a place to explore the positive side of life.

13
Finally, Positive News
http://www.positivenews.com
I've got great news for you. You'll find only good news here, all the time. Hallelujah!

14
Positive Vibrations
http://www.worldtrans.org/positive.html
This site is dedicated to positive trends and directions, good news, senseless optimism, creativity, humor and good feelings.

15
Psych Web

http://www.psychwww.com

To some degree, we're all psychologists. Here you'll find information for the psychologist within you.

16
Self-Help Psychology Magazine

http://www.shpm.com

Read an assortment of articles on self-help and get breaking news stories in the field of mental health. You can also subscribe to a free newsletter and participate in a discussion forum.

17
Service With a Click

http://www.thehungersite.com

You'll feel that you're doing something good when you click on this site, because a business sponsor will then pay to feed someone hungry in the world.

18
Creating Abundance

http://www.prosperityplace.com

Here you can learn all about the ins and outs of how to be more prosperous in your life. Prosperity means a lot more than just having money!

19
In Touch

http://www.intouchmag.com

The Intouch Online Magazine explores vital information about health, ecology, personal growth, professional development, creativity and wellness.

20
Exploring Mental Health

http://www.mhsource.com

Whether layperson or professional, you will find this to be an excellent resource for mental health information. There are lots of links covering an assortment of mental health issues.

21
Mending the Mind

http://www.mentalhelp.net
This award-winning guide to mental health, psychology and psychiatry online can provide lots of useful information.

22
Help is Here

http://www.nmha.org
The National Mental Health Association is dedicated to improving mental health of individuals and achieving victory over mental illness.

23
Exploring Mental Health

http://mentalhealth.about.com
Articles, forums, chat, newsletter and links for you to explore the many facets of mental health.

24
Stress No More

http://www.teachhealth.com
Read the online book "How to Survive Unbearable Stress," by Steven L. Burns, M.D., and learn how to manage your stress.

25
A Rehab Resource

http://www.naric.com
National Rehabilitation Information Center has a lot to share about disability and rehabilitation from its own collection of journal articles and from the results of federally-funded research projects.

26
Planet Psych

http://www.planetpsych.com
Learn about disorders, treatments and other topics in psychology. You might want to check out the self-help techniques, take a depression quiz, ask an expert or sign up for a newsletter.

27
Let's Talk Success
http://www.success-talk.com
This Internet audio broadcasting network provides live and on-demand programming in the areas of self-help and personal/professional development.

28
Managing Yourself
http://www.srg.co.uk
Go ahead, take the plunge and find out how to manage yourself and how to help lead others.

29
Are You Emotionally Intelligent?
http://www.enchantedmind.com/emote.htm
How well do you blend your head and your heart? Take an Emotional IQ Test, and see for yourself.

30
Personal Development
http://www.personal-development.com
A good place to visit for learning about personal development. It's nice to know we can keep on growing.

31
Non-Mainstream Alternatives
http://www.psyctc.org/mirrors/non-main/nonmain.htm
Looking for non-mainstream psychotherapy and counseling information? Here's your resource on the Internet.

32
Ride the Wave
http://www.thehalcyon.org
You can get linked and cruise to the many sites of the great thinkers in the fields of humanistic, transpersonal and quantum psychology.

33
New Times

http://www.newtimes.org
Enrich your life with a full range of cutting-edge articles in the field of personal and spiritual growth.

34
Power Learning

http://mailer.fsu.edu/~jflake/power.html
A worthwhile stop if you are interested in exploring sites about how you can improve your capacity to learn.

35
Heartmath

http://www.heartmath.org
This research and educational organization has developed simple, user-friendly tools people can use to relieve stress and break through to greater levels of personal balance, creativity and intuitive insight.

"The reason I'm successful is because I'm lucky.
But I didn't get lucky until I started
working 90 hours a week!"

36
Perspectives
http://www.mentalhelp.net/perspectives
This informative, monthly e-zine provides insight into today's mental health issues.

37
Conscious Net
http://www.consciousnet.com
You will find an assortment of mind-body-spirit information, services and products that can help enhance your life.

38
Sentient Times
http://www.sentienttimes.com
This magazine offers alternatives for personal and community transformation.

39
Explore New Concepts

http://www.conceptsmagazine.org

Here you can find a variety of articles on personal and spiritual growth.

40
Living Better for Less

http://www.stretcher.com

Your weekly resource for simple living.

41
Beyond Dreaming

http://i.am/somnio

Want to know how to be awake in your dreams? Learn about lucid dreaming at this site, and your dreams will never be the same again.

42
All About Hypnosis

http://www.hypnosis.com
http://www.hypnos.co.uk/hypnomag
If you would like to learn more about hypnosis, start with these sites.

43
Go Inside

http://www.goinside.com
"Go Inside" is an independent resource of international information. If you need blunt, insightful and ringing commentary on the world at large, then you need to "Go Inside."

44
A Journal of Consciousness

http://www.imprint.co.uk/jcs.html
The "Journal of Consciousness Studies" is a peer-reviewed journal that examines the study of consciousness in plain English.

CHAPTER II
TO YOUR HEALTH

45
Discover Health

http://www.discoveryhealth.com
Visit this informative site to find out about healthy living, men's health, women's health, news and more.

46
Health From A to Z

http://www.healthatoz.com
There is an abundance to explore about healthy lifestyles, health and wellness, diseases and conditions, health headlines and other topics.

47
To Your Health

http://www.yourhealth.com
You can find interesting stories here about today's health news headlines, or you may want to browse through a huge selection of articles on an assortment of health-related issues.

48
Here's to Wellness

http://www.wellweb.com
Wellness Web can help you find useful medical information, treatment options, research, how to select a health care provider, tips about healthy lifestyles and complementary treatment alternatives.

49
Assess Your Health

http://www.youfirst.com

This site asks, "Want to add years to your life? Find out how with a free personal health assessment." Sounds too good to be true, but it's worth a few minutes of your time.

50
Be the Best You Can

http://library.advanced.org/12153

"Bodies in Motion; Minds at Rest." This Web site is designed to improve your physical and mental health.

51
Holistic Healing

http://www.holisticmed.com

If you are interested in holistic medicine, this is a resource you will definitely want to check out.

52
Life Enrichment

http://www.earthmed.com

At this site, you can find health information and make contacts with people in the field of alternative medicine.

53
A Well of Health

http://www.healthwell.com

Log on to a healthier life. From aging well to workplace health, this site will assist with your lifestyle.

54
Health and Nutrition

http://www.hnbreakthroughs.com

Read articles about health and nutrition breakthroughs.

55
Health and Wellness Appraisal

http://alexian.hraonline.com

"Health and Wellness Appraisal" is an educational tool designed to pinpoint controllable health risk factors and provide you with suggestions for making positive lifestyle changes.

56
Fitness for All

http://www.fitnessfind.com
http://www.netsweat.com

If you're looking for fitness resources, these are comprehensive training guides on the Net.

57
Lets Get Complementary

http://nccam.nih.gov

The National Center for Complementary and Alternative Medicine evaluates alternative medical treatment modalities to determine their effectiveness.

58
Trimming Down

http://www.cyberdiet.com

http://www.dietwatch.com

These sites can inspire you and help you succeed with your weight loss goals.

59
Your Health Center

http://new.health-center.com

http://www.heal-all.com

At these sites, you will find a wealth of information about many facets of health and wellness.

60
Health is Wealth

http://www.sni.net/healthinfo

This site challenges old assumptions of illness and health and brings in some fresh ideas for you to ponder.

61
Honor Your Lungs

http://www.quitsmokingsupport.com
http://www.tobaccofreekids.org
Information and resources are available to assist you with smoking cessation.

62
Healthfinder

http://www.healthfinder.gov
This site is a useful gateway to the U.S. government's consumer health and human services information.

63
Sleep Net

http://www.sleepnet.com
Everything you wanted to ask about sleep but were too tired to ask.

64
Health, Wealth and Happiness

http://maxpages.com/debweb

Looking for health, wealth and happiness? You'll find insightful articles and Web sites to visit.

65
Healthy Way Magazine

http://www1.sympatico.ca/Contents/health

http://www1.sympatico.ca/healthyway/HEALTHYWAY/hway_mag.html

Learn about living a lifestyle of health and wellness, and find articles and other health information.

66
Thrive Online

http://www.thriveonline.com

Medical, fitness, nutrition, sexuality, weight and serenity are wellness topics addressed at Thrive Online.

67
Wellness Junction

http://www.wellnessjunction.com

Whether you're a consumer, professional or student, the junction has health and wellness information to assist you with your daily life. You can also sign up to get a weekly newsletter.

68
Body and Soul

http://homearts.com/depts/health/00dphec1.htm

Forums, chats, the latest news and research and great information on natural health and health-related issues.

69
Be Well

http://www.bewell.com

You can access a wealth of information about wellness for men, women, athletes, parents and seniors.

70
Alternative Medicine
http://www.alternativemedicine.com
Explore this database of more than 6,500 pages on alternative medicine and how to get and stay well.

71
Stay Healthy
http://www.stayhealthy.com
Stay healthy with the help of this portal site. It's a great resource for useful information about wellness.

72
Go For Health
http://www.athealth.com
At Health is an excellent mental health resource where you can find informative and educational articles and access a professional directory and treatment centers around the country.

73
Positive Health

http://www.positivehealth.com
Assume personal responsibility for your well-being, with this site as your assistant.

74
My Prime Time

http://www.myprimetime.com
Money, work, health and play are the areas of focus at this site. You can find some interesting articles to ponder.

75
Wellness Options

http://www.wellnessweb.com
You'll find lots of information about illness, complementary treatment options and tips about living healthy.

76
Healthy Living
http://healthyliving.women.com/hl/mbs
A wealth of information on total-body wellness, natural medicine and alternative treatments — nourishment for mind, body and spirit.

77
Live Life to Its Fullest
http://www.holisticzone.com
You can cruise the Holistic Zone for resources, recipes, exercises, guidelines and insights that can help you live life to its fullest.

78
The Life Pages
http://www.thelifepages.com
A great place to learn about wellness. Join in a discussion group and share how you think we can be healthier and make the world a better place.

79
Be E-Fit

http://www.efit.com

Send them a picture, and they will give you a "morphover." Learn how a diet and fitness plan could change your look and your life.

80
Twin Cities Wellness

http://www.tcwellness.com

A good place to visit if you are interested in alternative healthcare, body-mind medicine, spiritual well-being and the blending of holistic and Western medicine.

81
Share Guide

http://www.shareguide.com

Share Guide is a magazine focusing on holistic health, personal growth and environmental awareness.

82
Whole Health

http://www.WholeLifeHealth.com
For learning more about holistic living, make this a part of your life.

83
Conscious Choice

http://www.consciouschoice.com
The "Journal of Ecology and Natural Living" will provide you a lot of valuable information to explore.

84
Cultivate Your Energy

http://www.nqa.org
http://www.healing-tao.com
http://216.71.205.252
If you would like to learn about chikung/qigong, check out these sites. They're about healing and restoring balance through the cultivation of your life energy.

85
Flow With Yoga

http://www.yogaclass.com
http://www.yrec.org
Learn about yoga. It's not about effort; it's about flowing and allowing.

CHAPTER III
LIFT YOUR SPIRITS

86
Self-Worth

http://www.self-worth.com
You can get some inspiration delivered daily to your computer with the Motivational Mailer. This site encourages us to feel good about ourselves.

87
Visit Dr. Bernie

http://www.drbernie.com
Learn about Dr. Bernie's seven-themed "Guide for Living." From healing to spirituality, he can help.

88
Daily Encouragement
http://www.lifesupportsystem.com
Receive a free, daily e-mail message that is encouraging, thought-provoking, uplifting and often humorous.

89
The Humor Project
http://www.HumorProject.com
The Humor Project helps people get more "smileage" out of their lives and jobs by applying the practical, positive power of humor and creativity.

90
Heart Warmer
http://www.heartwarmers4u.com
These daily e-mail messages are designed to inspire you and provide insight on how people around the world are overcoming the everyday challenges they face.

91
Humor Matters
http://www.humormatters.com
Learn about humor and its relation to health and healing.

92
Mental Health Matters
http://www.mental-health-matters.com
Here you will find a directory for mental health and mental illness resources for professionals, clients and families.

93
Dr Ivan's Depression Central
http://www.psycom.net/depression.central.html
This site is a central clearinghouse for information on all types of depressive disorders and the most effective treatments.

94
Inspirational Stories
http://www.inspirationalstories.com
Inspirational stories can touch your heart and rekindle your soul. You will find some of them here.

95
Rainbow Garden
http://www.io.com/~rga/rainbow.html
This is a growing garden of positive thinking, recovery, spiritual wellness, wisdom and inspiration in the form of stories, parables, metaphors, poetry and quotes.

96
Get Motivated
http://www.greatday.com/motivate
Receive a daily motivational quote.

97
Refresh Your Spirit

http://www.allspirit.co.uk

This site is a place to refresh your spirit with an oasis of wonderful poetry and inspirational quotations.

98
For Seekers

http://www.seekermagazine.com

Hear the voices of everyday people sharing their stories, poems, art, music and articles. There is room to spare, so you can also become part of the content.

99
Depression Guide

http://www.pslgroup.com/DEPRESSION.HTM

Get the latest medical news and information on depression and related disorders.

100
Overcoming Depression

http://www.blarg.net/~charlatn/Depression.html

http://www.wingofmadness.com

For anyone suffering from depression, visit here to get some helpful information.

101
Depression 101

http://www.suite101.com/welcome.cfm/depression

This is an excellent site that features valuable information about the different aspects of depression. You can learn about treatment options and sign up for an online newsletter.

102
Motivating Moments

http://www.motivateus.com

Looking for inspiration? Here, you'll find motivational, inspirational, positive and success-oriented quotes. There is also a great section of motivational quotes submitted by teenagers.

103
Your Daily Jumpstart
http://www.neileskelin.com
Get a daily 200-word spark of personal motivation and inspiration.

104
Follow Your Dreams
http://www.followyourdreams.com
To help you follow your dreams, just follow the signs for motivation and inspiration.
There is also a place to share your inspirations and hear what others are dreaming.

105
Motivational Mecca
http://www.onlineconsulting.com/excite.html
This site provides a mecca of motivational and inspirational stories to ponder.

106
Help For Anxiety

http://www.algy.com/anxiety/index.shtml
You can visit this self-help network to learn about overcoming anxiety.

107
Panic No More

http://panicdisorder.about.com
This site is filled with lots of useful information and articles on stress, anxiety and panic disorders. There are also great links to other self-improvement sites.

108
Getting Over Trauma

http://www.trauma-pages.com/index.phtml
Here you can find a wealth of information about emotional trauma and traumatic stress, including post-traumatic stress disorder.

If you write down your goals 15 times every day, you can accomplish anything.

109
About Anxiety

http://www.adaa.org

The Anxiety Disorder Association of America promotes the prevention and cure of anxiety disorders and works to improve the lives of people who suffer from them.

CHAPTER IV
REBUILDING LIVES

110
Transformations
http://www.transformations.com/contents.html
Transformations is a site for self-help, support and recovery issues. Drop by a chat room or browse for other support and recovery information.

111
Habitsmart
http://www.habitsmart.com
Find useful information about identifying and managing addictive and problematic habitual behavior.

112
Leave the Bottle
http://www.alcoholics-anonymous.org
Everything you would like to know about AA can be found here. An assessment quiz as well as information for professionals is available.

113
Get Educated
http://www.nida.nih.gov/NIDAHome.html
The National Institute on Drug Abuse has a comprehensive site with updates on drug abuse education.

114
Addiction Resource Guide
http://www.hubplace.com/addictions
Here's a detailed directory of addiction treatment facilities in the U.S. and other parts of the world.

115
Recovery Network
http://www.recoverynetwork.com
This is a good source for prevention and recovery information that also features a chat room and a "Recovery Radio Show" live on the Web.

116
Smart Recovery
http://www.smartrecovery.org
Self-Management and Recovery Training (SMART) is a treatment approach with a support network for those seeking alternatives to the 12-Step treatment model.

117
Help For Families
http://www.Al-Anon-Alateen.org
Al-Anon is a worldwide organization that offers a self-help recovery program for family and friends of alcoholics.

118
Getting Informed
http://www.well.com/user/woa
This is an excellent resource for teachers, students and others who would like some up-to-date information and resources about alcohol and drug abuse.

119
Cocaine Anonymous
http://www.ca.org
CA offers a 12-Step recovery program for those suffering from cocaine addiction. It also lists phone numbers and Web sites for local chapters.

120
You Don't Have To Bet
http://www.gamblersanonymous.org
This resource helps individuals who have a gambling addiction. A directory for finding meetings in local areas is provided.

121
Holding Off Narcotics

http://www.na.org

Narcotics Anonymous is an international, community-based association of recovering drug addicts providing support for those in need.

122
Moderation Management

http://www.moderation.org

Do you want to cut back or quit drinking? This site has been designed for folks who say, "Yes, I do."

123
Grant Me the Serenity

http://www.open-mind.org

This site can be of help in exploring recovery options for various addictions, obsessions or compulsions.

124
Recovery Resources
http://www.recoveryresources.org
From personal stories to an abundance of recovery links, you're sure to find some assistance here.

125
Help and Hope
http://www.ncadd.org
The National Council on Alcoholism and Drug Dependence provides education, information, help and hope in the fight against alcohol and drug addiction.

126
Get Up To Date
http://www.health.org
The National Clearinghouse for Alcohol and Drug Information is said to be the world's largest resource for current information and materials concerning substance abuse.

127
Secular Recovery
http://www.unhooked.com
The online magazine of "Life Ring Secular Recovery" offers support and treatment of addiction as an alternative to the 12-Step model.

128
Personal Empowerment
http://members.aol.com/empower16/steps.htm
Empower yourself. "The 16 Steps to Personal Empowerment" is a flexible and holistic self-support alternative model for recovery.

129
Help for Eating Disorders
http://www.edap.org
EDAP is the nation's largest non-profit organization devoted to the awareness and prevention of eating disorders.

130
Something Fishy
http://www.something-fishy.org
Nothing is fishy here. You can learn about eating disorders and participate in a chat with other people.

131
Helping Hands
http://www.geocities.com/HotSprings/4192/index.htm
Receive support and information about eating disorders from people who have recovered or are in recovery.

132
Mirror, Mirror
http://www.mirror-mirror.org/eatdis.htm
Do you say "Mirror, mirror on the wall, who's the fattest one of all?" or "Mirror, mirror on the wall, who's the fairest one of all?" Get some thoughtful information about eating disorders.

133
Don't Hit

http://www.blainn.cc/abuse

Brian has an excellent resource for learning about domestic abuse patterns in relationships.

CHAPTER V
WOMEN ONLY

134
Woman's Health Interactive
http://www.womens-health.com
Here's an interactive learning environment where woman can explore and learn about physical health, mental health and wellness issues.

135
Moms Online
http://www.momsonline.com
Moms Online is a community of mothers created to support and educate other mothers about all stages of child rearing. Visit a chat room or sign up for an informative newsletter.

136
Babies Like Breastfeeding
http://www.lalecheleague.org
The La Leche League is dedicated to providing education, information, support and encouragement to women who want to breastfeed.

137
Single Moms
http://www.singlerose.com
A great educational and supportive online resource for single mothers. Chat or read articles on issues that single mothers face when raising children alone.

138
Woman as Sisters
http://women.weavingwebs.com/sister
This online book was written by women who share stories about their inner and outer lives as well as their spiritual journeys.

139
Woman Speak
http://www.voiceofwomen.com/VOWworld.html
Women tell their stories, discuss real issues and share hard-won wisdom.

140
The Voice of Woman
http://www.amazoncityradio.com
Visit here and listen to women speak on a Web radio station just for women.

141
A Place for Women
http://www.women.com
Here is a place for women to learn about health, well-being and more.

"Five years ago, my husband and I fell in love over the Internet. To celebrate our anniversary, we're finally going to meet face to face!"

142
Women's Wellness

http://www.wwn.on.ca
Articles and discussions of many issues that affect the daily lives of women are presented here.

143
Whispers for Woman

http://www.cyberpathway.com/whispers
An online magazine for woman to stay up to date and learn about new ways of thinking and being.

144
Woman Leaders Unite

http://www.wlo.org
This site is about women organizing for change through this activist group that empowers women in politics, media, society, the economy and cyberspace.

145
The Third Age
http://www.thirdage.com/guides/health/women
This is a great resource to educate and empower women about the honoring of the midlife journey of menopause.

146
Stepmoms
http://www.stepmothers.org
Women help women here, with emotional support and strategies for coping with the challenge of being a part of a step-parenting family.

147
The Second Wives Club
http://www.secondwivesclub.com
This online support group is dedicated to bringing second wives and stepmoms relevant information, encouragement and support within the realms of remarriage and stepfamily issues.

148
Redbook Online
http://www.redbook.women.com/rb
A good site for women to learn how to improve marriage, health and family life.

149
Leather Spinsters
http://www.leatherspinsters.com/ezine.html
This e-zine is enriching and dedicated to happily unmarried women, whom they refer to as the "leather spinsters."

150
Woman Today
http://www.womentodaymagazine.com
Woman Today Magazine is helping women around the world live life to its fullest, with topics from "advice" to "spirit."

151
Women's University

http://www.womensu.com
Learn and grow—the first virtual educational community by, for and about women—brings today's hottest workshop topics to busy women everywhere through the convenience of teleconference bridge technology.

152
Women's Health

http://www.nytimes.com/specials/women/whome
The New York Times is committed to keeping you up to date on women's health issues and concerns.

153
To Her Health

http://www.herhealth.com
Her Health Online is a holistic health magazine for women of all ages. One recent tip: "Give yourself a nice hot bubble bath today; you deserve it!"

154
Take Wellness to Heart

http://women.americanheart.org

The American Heart Association Women's Web site gives the facts on women's heart disease and stroke. Learn how lifestyle changes can lower those risks.

155
Women's Journeys

http://www.womensjourneys.com

Hear about many important issues women share from their heart at this place of personal empowerment.

156
Gifts of Speech

http://gos.sbc.edu .

Read what great women thinkers think. This site is dedicated to preserving and creating access to speeches made by influential, contemporary women.

CHAPTER VI
MEN ONLY

157
Fathering

http://fatherwork.byu.edu
Here you will find stories, ideas and activities to encourage good fathering. You can even share your personal stories.

158
Boot Camp for New Dads

http://www.newdads.com
A great resource for new and soon-to-be dads. Learn the ropes from veteran dads who themselves received support from the site.

159
Fathering Magazine
http://www.fathermag.com
An online magazine for fathers that includes feature articles, true stories, news headlines, expert advice and more.

160
How to Be A Better Dad
http://www.fathers.com
The National Center for Fathering inspires and equips men to be better fathers. It offers practical resources for dads to improve their fathering skills.

161
Men and Grief
http://www.vix.com/menmag/menmag/mengrief.htm
An excellent site for men to read articles about men and grief. You can also find poetry and men's stories.

162
Father's World
http://www.fathersworld.com
The mission here is to promote and celebrate fatherhood and family as the leading source of information, resources, support and education for all types of fathers and their families.

163
Male Health Center
http://www.malehealthcenter.com
Dr. Goldberg provides you with a holistic approach to men's health issues.

164
Forums in A Mans Life
http://apps.manslife.com/forum
Cars, women, money and many more forums are available for your participation.

165
Men's Issues Page

http://www.vix.com/pub/men
Men's issues are classified for you here, using an encyclopedia approach. Browse the issues at your leisure.

166
Coalitions for Fathers

http://www.acfc.org
http://users.erols.com/afc
These coalitions for fathers support the equal rights of fathers and discuss issues such as the importance of shared parenting time and joint custody.

167
Warrior Soul

http://www.geocities.com/~waymac
What male issues confront you? This site is a source of information and support for men and the issues that confront them.

168
Achilles Heel
http://www.achillesheel.freeuk.com
Achilles Heel is a magazine for and about men.

169
Men in Movement
http://www.castlebooks.com/search.html
Despite all the search engines on the Net, there is a need for this one designed just for men.

CHAPTER VII
FAMILY LIFE

170
The Gift Of Parenting

http://www.abcparenting.com
Enjoy the gift of parenting, and learn a lot about it at this site.

171
Family Education

http://www.familyeducation.com/home
Dedicated to children's learning, this site will assist in educating kids and empowering parents. It is an online community center for parents to connect with experts and other parents.

172
Connect For Kids

http://www.connectforkids.org

Connect for Kids is a virtual encyclopedia of information for adults who want to make their communities better places for kids.

173
Infertility Support

http://www.resolve.org

The mission of this national fertility organization is to provide timely, compassionate support and information to individuals who are experiencing infertility.

174
Children and Youth with Disabilities

http://www.nichcy.org

The National Information and Referral Center provides details on disabilities and disability-related issues for families, educators, and other professionals.

175
Parenting Center

http://www.childmagazine.com
From pregnancy to travel, Child magazine is there for parents.

176
Baby Place

http://www.baby-place.com
Issues that affect you as a parent are discussed here. You can also vote on such topics as, "What morning sickness treatment helped you the most?"

177
Parent Soup

http://www.parentsoup.com
Find discussion boards, live chats and lots of information on a variety of pregnancy and parenting issues.

"You're getting pretty good
at this stress management thing."

178
The Parents Page
http://www.efn.org/~djz/birth/babylist.html
Issues that every parent will have to address are discussed here.

179
Parents Place
http://www.parentsplace.com
From pregnancy to parenting, you will find useful information, chat rooms and discussion boards.

180
Baby Center
http://www.babycenter.com
From preconception to toddler, the center has information, advice and a newsletter for you.

181
Helpful Parenting
http://www.npin.org
The National Parent Information Network provides useful details to parents and those who work with parents. NPIN says, "We believe that well-informed families are likely to make good decisions about raising and educating their children."

182
Adolescence Directory
http://www.education.indiana.edu/cas/adol/adol.html
This guide explores a variety of adolescent issues and is a great place for teens to hang out and access a variety of resources that are designed for them.

183
Parents, Teens and Kids
http://www.ala.org/parents
The American Library Association provides an abundance of Internet resources for parents, teens and kids, including over 700 sites.

184
Learning Disabilities

http://www.ldonline.org
Learning Disabilities Online is an interactive guide for parents, teachers and children. There is a lot of helpful information and a KidZone for children to explore.

185
Attention Deficit Disorder

http://www.chadd.org
This site is for children and adults with Attention Deficit Disorder and for those who work with them. Make sure you check out Attention! Magazine.

186
4 Kids

http://www.4kids.org
This is the quickest shot to the coolest spots. Children, parents and teachers can explore a variety of educational Web sites.

187
Kids Health

http://www.kidshealth.org
Read a large assortment of articles written by medical experts about the physical
and emotional well-being of children and teens.

188
Go Family

http://family.go.com
This online magazine will give you expert advice, chat rooms, local resources and
helpful monthly articles on child development, health and parenting.

189
Family Village

http://www.familyvillage.wisc.edu
Family Village is a global community that integrates information and resources on
the Internet for persons with cognitive or other disabilities. It is also helpful for
their families and for those that provide them services.

190
Children's Challenges

http://www.aacap.org

It's important for parents and families to understand behavioral, emotional and mental disorders of children. This very professional site can assist.

191
Overcoming Adversity

http://resilnet.uiuc.edu

Resilience Net offers information and resources to help children and families overcome adversities.

192
Children's Television Workshop

http://www.ctw.org

This site has plenty of informative articles from Sesame Street Parents about pre-schoolers' physical, emotional and intellectual development. Children can also explore online activities.

193
Family Web Corner
http://users.sgi.net/~cokids

At this site, you can find articles and links on education in America, health and nutrition, parenting, consumer information, safety and more. Suggestions for what you can do with your children at home are also provided.

194
Kids Source
http://www.kidsource.com

Experience in-depth, timely education and healthcare information that can make a difference in the lives of parents and their children. Get free, age-appropriate newsletters to help busy parents raise and educate their children.

195
Principles of Parenting
http://www.humsci.auburn.edu/parent

You'll find professional and educational articles in such areas as "Strengthening the Parent," "Developing the Caring Child" and "Developing the Strong Child."

196
Stepfamily Information
http://www.stepfamilyinfo.org
Step into an educational site that proposes ways co-parents can prevent divorce while promoting stepfamily health, security and satisfaction.

197
Parenting Toolbox
http://www.parentingtoolbox.com
This is a great place to go to put some nontraditional parenting skills that help promote healthy family life in your parenting toolbox.

198
About Our Kids
http://www.aboutourkids.org
Issues about parenting and children's mental health are addressed at this site.

199
Voices of Adoption

http://www.ibar.com/voices

Read articles about the many issues and facets of adoption. While you're here, you can also enjoy personal stories about adoption by those who have experienced it.

200
I Am Your Child

http://www.iamyourchild.org

"I Am Your Child" is a national awareness campaign to make early childhood development a top priority in our nation. At the site, you can find useful parenting information and expert advice.

201
Rosemond Speaks

http://www.rosemond.com

John, a well-known parenting expert, provides you with daily tips and articles about the important role of parenting.

202
Teen Advice Online

http://www.teenadvice.org

Its stated mission is "To provide support for teenage problems through a network of peers around the globe."

CHAPTER VIII
AGING GRACEFULLY

203
Grand Times

http://www.grandtimes.com
Enjoy this weekly Internet magazine for seniors. Grand Times celebrates life's opportunities and examines life's challenges.

204
Senior Pages

http://www.seniorpages.com
http://www.ageofreason.com
No matter how old we get, we can always be young at heart. Information and links specifically related to issues for seniors can be found at this site.

205
The Good Life

http://www.goodlifemag.com

The Good Life magazine approaches aging with a positive attitude. It satisfies the thirst of people who have turned forty for clues about aging.

206
Options at 50 Plus

http://www.OptionsUSA.com

Options is an online resource for folks who are fifty plus. Baby boomers, you are also welcome here.

207
Grow in the Flow

http://www.agingresearch.org

The Alliance For Aging Research helps people gain access to the latest scientific information that can empower them to live more healthy and independent lives.

208
My Mother and Alzheimer's

http://www.zarcrom.com/users/yeartorem
This wonderful, heartfelt site is very useful for anyone who has a loved one suffering from Alzheimer's.

209
Aging Parents

http://www.agenet.com
Use this information and referral network to bridge the distance between aging parents and adult children.

210
Health and Wellness

http://www.aarp.org/indexes/health.html
AARP has a wealth of information for seniors. Learn about a variety of practical topics related to aging, health and wellness.

211
Elderweb

http://www.elderweb.com

Visit the oldest and largest eldercare sourcebook on the Web. This is a great place to cruise the thousands of links to eldercare and longterm care information on legal, financial, medical and housing issues.

212
For Seniors Only

http://www.seniors-site.com

An assortment of useful health and aging information for seniors and their children is available at this site. You can even e-mail your questions to advisors.

213
Support for Caregivers

http://www.caregiving.com

This site offers you access to the support, information and resources you need when you are caring for an aging relative.

CHAPTER IX
DIFFICULT TRANSITIONS

214
Approaching Death

http://pompeii.nap.edu/books/0309063728/html
"Approaching Death: Improving Care at the End of Life" is an online book that addresses many of the issues related to end-of-life care.

215
Growth House

http://www.growthhouse.org
Consult this excellent educational resource for addressing issues concerning death, dying, grief and bereavement.

216

Hospice

http://www.nho.org
http://www.HospiceFoundation.org
Hospice is a special kind of care that provides comfort and support to clients and families in the final stages of terminal illness. Learn all about it and how to find a local chapter.

217

Death and Dying

http://www.death-dying.com
Great articles and information about death, dying and grieving are here. This is a good support resource with wonderful sections for kids and teens dedicated to helping them through the loss of a loved one.

"Our latest chip contains Ginkgo Biloba to help improve your computer's memory and mental focus!"

218
Support for Grieving

http://www.groww.com
Peer groups in this chat room environment provide support for people who are in the process of grieving.

219
Crisis, Grief and Healing

http://www.webhealing.com
Discuss, chat or browse this site to understand and honor different paths for healing strong emotions.

220
Compassionate Friends

http://www.compassionatefriends.org
The mission here is to assist families in the positive resolution of grief following the death of a child.

221
Widownet

http://www.fortnet.org/~goshorn

This is an information and self-help resource by widows and widowers for anyone who has suffered the loss of a life partner.

222
Learn About AIDS

http://www.thebody.com

This site is designed to demystify HIV/AIDS and its treatment, and to improve patients' quality of life.

223
Mothers in Sympathy and Support

http://www.misschildren.org

This is a safe haven where parents can face their grief after the loss of a child.

224
Share

http://www.nationalSHAREOffice.com

This organization provides valuable services to caregivers and parents whose children have died. The site includes links, helpful resources and access to their support network.

225
Journey of Hearts

http://www.kirstimd.com

For anyone who has ever experienced a loss or significant life change, this site can help support the grieving process.

226
Before I Die

http://www.wnet.org/archive/bid

PBS explores the medical, ethical and social issues surrounding end-of-life care in America today. Through real life stories, a refreshing perspective emerges.

227
Grief Share

http://www.griefshare.org

This is a special place where you can find help as you grieve the loss of a family member or friend. You can search the database to find a griefshare group near you.

CHAPTER X
RELATIONSHIPS

228
Lets Relate

http://www.Relationship-Talk.com
At this site, you can get advice and learn how to have healthy relationships, deal with difficult ones and cope with loss and pain.

229
Marriage Enrichment

http://www.marriageenrichment.com
This association promotes resources to strengthen marital relationships and enhance personal growth and family wellness. Try out the marital enrichment exercise every week.

230
Relationship Journey
http://www.relationshipjourney.com
Learn about forming successful, healthy relationships and ways to support your personal development.

231
Marriage Builders
http://www.marriagebuilders.com
Dr. Harley will introduce you to some of the best ways to overcome marital conflict and restore love.

232
Create Positive Relationships
http://www.positive-way.com
Find information here that can help you improve and enhance any relationship. Learn about creating positive, lasting and loving relationships.

233
Divorce Room

http://www.heartchoice.com/divorceroom

Hosted by people who have been through it, this site offers resources and practical suggestions about surviving the challenge of divorce.

234
Support Is Here

http://www.support-group.com

People with health, personal and relationship issues can share their experiences through an extensive listing of bulletin boards and online chats.

235
To the Rescue

http://www.relationshipweb.com

Get first aid for relationships, with a directory of helpful relationship links, discussion forums and help on affairs, marriage, dating, divorce, addiction, abuse, breakups and much more.

236
Love Advice
http://www.loveadvice.com
Dr. Tracy Cabot offers lots of information and advice on relationships. Go ahead, read one of her informative articles, or even ask her a question.

237
I'm Not Okay When You're Not Okay
http://www.artdsm.com/recover/preface.html
Here is a valuable resource guide about codependency for adult children of dysfunctional families.

238
Couples Place
http://www.couples-place.com
The goal here is "To help people succeed at marriage and other couple relationships by providing information, skills-training and encouragement, and by offering a confidential learning community where people can share openly and benefit from each others' experiences."

239
Stepfamily Support

http://www.stepfamily.net

If you are in a stepfamily, use this site to find useful information that can help you better understand some of the challenges that may be at hand. You can also send in your questions and receive expert advice.

240
Miraculous Relationships

http://www.geocities.com/Athens/Delphi/1171/relationships.html

Here is a free, 52-lesson online course on how to develop miraculous relationships that keep the flame of love and happiness alive.

241
Light Your Fire

http://www.lightyourfire.com

Dr. Ellen Kreidman will help you learn important information about relationships and yourself, share your thoughts, make new friends and have a great time.

242
Love is Great

http://www.LoveisGreat.com
Hear more about the philosophy that says, "Love is that condition in which the happiness of another person is essential to your own."

243
Love Net

http://www.lovenet.com
How would you like free relationship advice, articles, dating tips and free photo personals? This is the place.

244
Relationship Forums

http://www.net-love.org
Get your relationship questions answered at the advice forum. You can also participate in an open discussion forum or check out the personal ads.

245
Building Healthy Relationships
http://www.valhallamoon.com
Let Kim and Gary provide you with a relaxed, but philosophical, approach to relationships. They have done a great job, and the Web site design provides a peaceful feeling.

246
Self-Therapy
http://www.execpc.com/~tonyz
Enjoy learning about yourself and the dynamics of your relationship.

247
Whole Family Center
http://www.wholefamily.com
How do we relate? Here you will find expert advice and resources for every member of the family.

CHAPTER XI
NURTURING THE SPIRIT

248
A Healing Place

http://www.ahealingplace.org
This site proclaims, "Healing is a lesson in understanding. The requirements of understanding are an open mind, an open heart and good information. You bring the former, A Healing Place can provide the latter."

249
Inspired Living

http://www.inspiredinside.com
Educational, informational, motivational and inspirational articles, stories, discussion groups, resources and support are here to help you consciously create the life you would like.

250
Awareness Magazine
http://www.awarenessmag.com
This is a magazine devoted to improving your life and the life of our planet. You can read current articles or go all the way back to the previous century.

251
Evolutionary Ventures
http://www.evolutionaryventures.com
Evolutionary Ventures is dedicated to the co-creation and celebration of a compassionate and sustainable world.

252
Phenomenal News
http://www.phenomenews.com
This is a really phenomenal resource for the metaphysical, holistic health and alternative-minded thinkers. Read articles or listen to the Net radio station.

"Yes, I know the secret to happiness
and I'll reveal it to the highest bidder on Ebay!"

253
InnerSelf

http://www.innerself.com
Columns, lots of articles, chats and many other resources can help us be in touch
with ourselves.

254
Inner Edge

http://www.inneredge.com
The Inner Edge is a forum for sharing stories and practical wisdom about living
your spirituality at the workplace.

255
Pathways Magazine

http://www.pathwaysmag.com
Check this out if you would like an informative mind-body-sprit, alternative
medicine and new age resource. You'll find information on topics ranging all the way
from "acupressure" to "vision."

256
Wisdom Network

http://www.wisdomnetwork.com
Wisdom TV and Radio Networks has plans to get us in the very best shape of our lives — physically, mentally, emotionally and spiritually.

257
New Dimensions

http://www.newdimensions.org
New Dimensions Radio explores social, environmental and spiritual frontiers through interviews with many of today's foremost thinkers, scientists and creative artists.

258
Awakening

http://www.sages-way.com
Here you can learn about the trances of everyday life. In other words, "When we give ourselves permission to examine our trances of everyday life, we discover who we are not, and this allows us to get closer to experiencing who we really are."

259
Common Boundary

http://www.commonboundary.org
Common Boundary is a nonprofit educational organization dedicated to exploring the sources of meaning in human experience and examining the relationships between psychology, spirituality and creativity. Enjoy the insightful articles.

260
The Center for Visionary Leadership

http://www.visionarylead.org
This center features nationally-known authors, social innovators and citizen dialogues for transformational change and inner development.

261
Voluntary Simplicity

http://www.slnet.com
Living simply can solve many problems. Learn exactly how to do it from the Simple Living Network.

262
An Internet Retreat
http://www.teleport.com/~interlud

This is a place to renew the spirit online and to experience a few moments of peace, composure and mental expansion. Check out the thought of the day, meditations and poems.

263
Global Renaissance Alliance
http://www.renaissancealliance.org

Many of the leaders in the fields of self-improvement and spiritual enhancement belong to this organization. Learn more about them here.

264
Positive Future
http://www.futurenet.org

Positive Futures Network is a nonprofit organization dedicated to supporting peoples' active engagement in creating a more sustainable, just and compassionate world. You can also read "Yes! A Journal of Positive Futures" here.

265
The Inspirational Center

http://www.inspire.org
Here you can find inspirational articles, columns, sharing and networking to support you on your spiritual journey.

266
Spirit at Work

http://www.spiritatwork.com
This site provides articles and a newsletter that focus on ideas for transforming the workplace so that creativity and compassion are emphasized.

267
Deepak Chopra

http://www.chopra.com
Dr. Chopra states, "The essence of all we offer is the recognition that the universe is a dynamic web of energy and information." Enjoy all the information at this site.

268
Intuition Network

http://www.intuition.org
The purpose of Intuition Network is to help create a world in which all people feel encouraged to cultivate and use their inner, intuitive resources. You can also read the transcripts from the "Thinking Allowed" PBS television series.

269
Feng Shui

http://www.qi-whiz.com
This site is dedicated to helping Feng Shui shed its snake-oil-and-incense image. You can access other Feng Shui sites from here and learn everything about the art of environmental arrangement.

270
Spiritual Growth

http://www.spiritualgrowth.com
You'll find explanations of spirituality, articles, forums and more about reawakening the spirit and nourishing the soul.

271
Matters of the Spirit
http://www.concentric.net/~conure/spirit.shtml
This is a good place to chill out and cruise through stories, quotes and essays about spiritual transformation.

272
Zen Stories
http://www.rider.edu/users/suler/zenstory/zenstory.html
Live and learn from this collection.

273
Concepts for Consideration
http://www.insyncnews.com
Explore provocative concepts for personal growth and expanded awareness, and read articles that can broaden your perspective or challenge your mind.

274
Thou Art That

http://www.thouartthat.com
This is a great alternative-minded site for exploring and challenging the conditioning of society. You'll find contributions from numerous well-known thinkers who may challenge what you think.

275
Many Paths

http://www.manypaths.com
This site is designed to assist people in their journey through life. You can explore an abundance of personal and spiritual growth information here.

276
Sage Place

http://www.sageplace.com
Sage Place is here to support you on your journey of healing and exploration of issues related to the wholeness of the mind, body, spirit and environment. While you're there, read the inspirational words of Chief Seattle.

277
Institute of Noetic Sciences

http://www.noetic.org
This organization has been at the forefront of research and education in consciousness and human potential for the last twenty-five years. It states, "Perhaps the only limits to the human mind are those we believe in."

278
Learn About Wisdom

http://www.isn.net/info/wisdompg.html
Wisdom is the ability to make sound choices and good decisions. Wisdom is also intelligence shaped by experience, information softened by understanding.

279
Enrich Your Soul

http://www.soullife.com
Get your free self-guided worksheets and exercises to help you grow psychologically and express your human potential.

280
Co-Creation
http://www.cocreation.org
This site serves to forge community and disseminate social innovations now working in all fields of human endeavor. Its stated purpose is to help discover the ever-evolving design for a positive future.

281
Tools for Transformation
http://www.trans4mind.u-net.com
The goal at this site is to use personal development resources to make us more aware of our true identities.

282
Celestine
http://www.celestinevision.com/main.html
Here you will find ongoing spiritual discussions and ideas about raising spiritual awareness throughout the world. Join in the conversation.

283
Zukav Speaks

http://www.zukav.com
Learn what Gary Zukav has to say about spiritual growth and social transformation, for example: "Our new goals are authentic power—the alignment of the personality with the soul—and a planet without conflict."

284
Colorado Nexus

http://hologram.net/nexus
Nexus is a leading voice in holistic health and natural living; from "herbs" to "workaholism," you'll find it here.

285
Thoughts Beneath the Trees

http://www.vantagequest.org/trees
Go here for some intellectually stimulating essays on transpersonal (esoteric mental experience) psychology.

286
Vision Magazine
http://www.visionmagazine.com
Categorized by earth, mind, heart, politics and future, Vision Magazine is about offering a model for a more conscious, peaceful and healthy world.

287
The Pursuit Of Balance
http://www.balancequest.com
Let BalanceQuest be your guide to high-quality information and materials for pursuing happiness and greater satisfaction in living.

288
Spirit Site
http://www.spiritsite.com
Here you will find a collection of resources for the spiritual path, such as excerpts from spiritual writings, online discussion forums and a gallery of audio and art selections with spiritual themes.

289
Spirit In the Smokies

http://www.spiritinthesmokies.com

Enjoy first-person transformational stories and interviews in the sprit of conscious evolution, joy and the celebration of life.

290
The Essence of Reality

http://www.nehrer.net

Thomas Daniel Nehrer, this site's proprietor says, "Enter with an open mind, and leave with a clear awareness of how life works."

CHAPTER XII
GETAWAYS FOR GROWTH

291
Esalen Institute

http://www.esalen.org
This classic center for alternative education is a forum for transformational practices, a restorative retreat, a worldwide networking of seekers and a place to renew the spirit.

292
Body/Mind/Spirit Expo

http://www.bodymindspiritexpo.com
Shop the world's best exhibitors and merchants in natural products, alternative healing and personal growth expositions and markets. Also, learn about expos around the country.

293
All About Retreats

http://www.allaboutretreats.com
Look up retreat facilities and conference centers to find workshops that align with
your interests.

294
Time For a Getaway

http://www.retreatsonline.com
These getaways range from business to spiritual retreats anywhere in the world.
There's even a section for exotic retreats.

295
Healing Retreats

http://www.healingretreats.com
Healing Retreats & Spas Magazine gives you great ideas on where to go for a
healing holiday. Make a selection by state or type of retreat.

296
Grow While You Have Fun

http://www.frommers.com/novel/resorts

Let Frommer assist you if you're seeking more out of a vacation. How about resorts that can stretch your mind and change your life?

297
Travel Naturally

http://www.naturalusa.com

"Natural Home and Travel Guide" will help you explore some interesting and unique travel options.

298
Healthy Travel

http://www.healthytravel.net

Just looking at this site will make you want to get away. With this healthy alternative to conventional travel, you'll find cruises, spas, retreats, educational adventures and spiritual journeys.

299
Holistic Studies

http://omega-inst.org

Here are various workshops, retreats and conferences in health, psychology, relationships, professional development, spirituality and more, conducted by many of the innovators of self-development.

300
Seminar Master

http://www.seminarmaster.com

There are so many seminars in such diverse categories here. Make a visit, and identify the ones that will assist you in your search for growth and knowledge.

Index (by Site Number)

Index (by Site Number)

INDEX (BY SITE NUMBER)

The Incredible Newsletter

If you are enjoying this book, you can also arrange to receive a steady stream of more "incredible Internet things," delivered directly to your e-mail address.

The Leebow Letter, Ken Leebow's weekly e-mail newsletter, provides new sites, updates on existing ones and information about other happenings on the Internet.

For more details about *The Leebow Letter* and how to subscribe, visit us at:

WWW.300INCREDIBLE.COM